A Mental Rose Series

A Mental Rose Series

❧

THE IMPERFECTIONS OF US

Tricia LM, B.A., M.A., M.S.Ed
&
T. Monk

T. Monk

Tri-State L.E, LLC

1

❧

THE IMPERFECTIONS OF US:
A Collection of Poems
First Edition

AUTHORS
TRICIA LM & T. MONK

~~~~~~~~~~~~~

This book is dedicated to, first and foremost, the Lord above, who has guided me through all the amazing and devastating times, as narrated within.

My favorites in the whole world- "SeaShells of Asia." Remember that you are God's Chosen Ones: Be wise, be smart, be beautiful, and know that you are powerful, and will accomplish all your dreams.

Family- Thank you for being my support circle.

Lastly, to all the triumphs, loss, loves, and haters—result in continual motivation!

~~~~~~~~~~~~~

Self-Published

Library of Congress Catalog

LM, Tricia

The Imperfections of Us: A Collection of Poems/

Tricia LM, T.Monk, 1st Ed.

English Language- Poetry/Free Verse

ISBN: 979-8-9855563-1-5

Preface

I live in my thoughts. I wear a life sized ski mask everyday; to mask my true thoughts and feelings. Why? Maybe I'm crazy or confused, but for some reason I feel my ways of conduct are very popular among poor urban blacks across the country. Why are we programmed to the extent of predictability? Do we disregard our predestined destiny? Is there any originality amongst us, and if so, where can it be found? If it can't be found then what's the solution?

Some believe that the bible speaks of blacks when it explains of the cursed people. If that's true, then that explains why black people, my people, are so damn intimidated by the evitable, and why I have turned to myself for all the answers.

Take note of the structure herein—- for a mere reflection of the evolution of time and the sentiments aligned.

These are my thoughts, once repressed, now released.

Keylock

You got my mind on keylock,

Trying to think beyond the average spectrum,

Illusions appearing as solutions,

Finding myself confused, used, and abused.

Your manipulations brings me temporary simulation.

What's your prize for keeping me disguised, disguised from your lies and true ties?

I envision my escape, only resulting in the awareness of my state.

I want out, need a resolution.

This pain is endless, frightening, it's so defying.

Knowing it's not love makes it all the more distressful.

Internal blockade of emotions, restrict the sensations of my keylocked mind.

You're selfish with my freedom, envious of my potential, and threatened by my strength.

No longer will I sustain my status of being keylocked in your circle of betrayal.

Do you even know your portrayal?

Camouflage

Emotions Derived from Camouflage

I think I love you,

I know I love you.

I love your every way.

The imperfections of your style are all so right.

The distance of your thoughts, identify your true identity.

The mysteriousness of your ways keeps me curious to the hidden you.

I think I love,

I know I love you.

I love your very scent.

Pure Hugo Boss, just cause you're a boss!

Leaving behind the sensations of your presence, only to have me wonder of your latter moves.

Smooth simulations of your aroma; have me dependent on your every appearance.

I think I love you,

I know I love you.

I love your humor; disguising me from the ugly truths of our reality.

Let me remain in this bliss, blissful vibrations of laughter, tenderness, and explorations.

I think I love you,

I know I love you.

I love you till the point it hurts.

Sounding as if the record was played once before, but instead, you're the new lead.

Play, play, and play some more, this sweet melody till the numbness subsides; temporary unconsciousness of this feeling called love.

I think I love you,

I know I love you for sure.

Sweet Sixteen

Dear Mr. Monk, (12/12/06)

You asked me last night to write a poem,

But every time I sit, breath, and clear my head, it's you I think about.

I want to find the perfect words to tell you, you make me smile,

Especially, when your tender lips kiss my eyes.

I find it essential to remind you, you were my sweet sixteen.

Reminiscing now on how much patience you had with me.

Maybe in this poem I should say something like I love to see the glow in your eyes.

But, all I can envision are those night stars on the bus rides to Clinton.

Our dates begin Friday nights and ends with Sunday kites; oh, how life doesn't seem right without my Monday-Saturday kites in the mail.

Anxious to hold you for eternity,

But, a deep power kiss is what I'm yearning for.

Descriptive Tales

Words can't describe the feelings that I vibe,

Your touch is a never-ending feel, sensation, motion, and tension in my veins.

I want you to stay, divine timing between you and I.

Your words are emotions that surface in my mind.

Repression, digression all extract from the past. Understanding the distance of time, recognizing the faults of life, move fast, but slow, as I recollect the moments.

T-N-T

Your love is...

flexible, yielding to the gentlest touch,

mildness, more joyful than the silliest pup.

Lucky,

is the name of the man, you struggle, or fight for.

A pugilist, lucky must choose the right door.

The left, is the remainder,

an inauspicious, bad move.

Our minds aren't bound

by borders, seas, time,

commitment doesn't see time

seen or unseen.

My mind, is with you,

more than with me.

Things moved quickly,

equipped with punctual wisdom,

past our years,

both of us scared,

abodes in different spheres,

zones, blissful tears

alone but peered,

paired when we meet,

you pear'd cause you sweet,

who dare to defeat?

Caribbean Queen

Away and confused, like, a lighthouse light,
burning during the day, in sunlight's rays,
burnt out by night,
look for a way, to find my way,
which way is that?
Follow my heart's lead, it beats, like the drums
or the sunshine,
I found my Caribbean coast
So close, but so far
wickedly great, so far, the odd and a weirdo,
escaped into bliss,
blindness, innocence, vacations to institutions
work week brunches,
A new wave of punches, punctures stabs at my heart, broke the drum,
sun went down, caught a plane, are we done?
Away and confused like a lighthouse,
talking to the waves crashing into it
on the most awkward of days.
Butterfly or colorful caterpillar,
patterns don't exist, no matter how long it appears, it was only a day,
up all night looking for my way!

Character

Your scent, your touch is everlasting, like the words of a favorite book.
Indulging some more, seeking a deeper meaning.
Questing for the captivity of your heart.
Road maps, navigations, all have rerouted.
Your spontaneity is inexplicable, wondrous as to which human trait it
replicates.
Mental devotion,
Sole alienation, until I complete my task of identifying your intricate
character.

The Question of Promiscuity

I love one,

but I want him.

I want him.

I want him to want and possess ownership of every part of me.

Forgetting all the negativity that surrounds him, me, our situation.

I want him.

I want him to play mind games, attracting my soul.

Spitting verses that rhyme with seduction.

I want him.

I want him to kiss my lips like I'm the women of his dreams; the true one he desires, more like adores.

Bite my tongue, wet my lips, separately, reminding me of your golden breath.

I want him.

I want him to create internal eruptions with his tender touches on my neck, down to the forefront of my nipples.

Lick me, suck me, like the bees of a beehive.

Tender, tender, tender.

Ummm, make me aware that you adore me.

I want him.

I want him to take his time with my true and solely hidden treasure. Caress her, announce your presence. Tour her gently with your fingers.

In, out, in, out, in, out.

Circle your tongue around her, ensuring your arrival is anticipated.

In, out, in, out, in, out.

Then, using the irrefutable symbol of masculinity,

dominate my shining gem with all the strength of your inner passion.

Once our climax is reached,

I want him more.

I want him to say he loves me, as I do him.

I want him,

I want him to one day know of this, my fantasy I pray he will fulfill.

Expiration Date

Flowers, singers, sadden faces, colorless clothes, jumbled languages, poems, speeches, stylish hair, musical tones, bowed heads, fidgeting fingers, sobs, old ages, minimal young faces, slugged walks and postures, forgotten tales, shortened laughs, small meals, watered eyes_____, I envision my death.

Sanity's Reasoning

I feel far from sane; but what's its metric measures?

Insanity defines my present state.

State of depression, of fears, tears, anger, and other emotions, -all those that are contrast to happiness.

I want and seek refuge, but result in the empty dungeon of myself.

My mind has refused me, betrayed me to life, leaving me to solve this equation of relativity.

I reason the dreadful act of suicide, as it appears a rapid solution. However, my insanity recalls the fear of self-mutiny.

I love to hate myself, wondering why this mental self- defecation has consumed me.

The Movement

I'm the movement,
the motion,
Chemistry,
the potion of life,
oceanly deep,
my sword is the light,
My brain scopes it all,
my eyes staring,
your not focused at all.
We beefin with the Pharroh,
who got his finger on the trigger,
our face on the barrel,
trying to blow us away...
What's my name?
The Wizard, Genus,
A Jedi, the Phenoix,
the lessons, the Jacksons,

the captain, the seamen,
on the eggs of the soul,
made the pop,
a movement, anything that explodes on ya block,
The Martins, the Malcolms,
The Ali's, the bout won,
We history without them,
no history without them.
I'm the first and infinite
Sorahs and Cornithians,
Horace,
But I keep the torch,
like Olympians,
Brain causes earthquakes,
enlightened in the cell,
a cage is my birthplace,
Asiatic first take,
cream of the planet,
never perpetrate.
System wanna dead me,
cops want lead in me,
my third eye,
two hours, three miles ahead of me.
Pedigree alone,
is a status and a symbol,
I'm self-evident, knowledge seed, two dimples,
I'm like the Ock's, the dreds,
Panthers and the fighters,
The Q's, Alpha's, Kappa's
United.
The source and start,
mist and the fog,
the smoke in the fire,
Bish me allah

I'm made of math and science,
rallies and riots,
treason defiance,
seas full of pirates,
bred of a lion,
bear and a shark,
I'm the balcony, Tennessee, Dr. King
the mark,
I'm the chalk on the park-
drawn around a homicide,
I'm the salt in the tears,
every time a mother cries.
I'm the movement,
the motion,
Chemistry,
the potion of life,
oceanly deep,
my sword is the light,
My brain scopes it all,
my eyes staring,
your not focused at all.
We beefin with the Pharroh,
who got his finger on the trigger,
our face on the barrel,
trying to blow us away...
Once again we got the blade,
they got the grip on the handle,
what we do is a crime,
and what they do is a scandal,
we get juries,
they get panels,
of colleagues, parents, partners,
who all lie,
Administration looking for a fall guy,

to hold the blame.
In the hood,
they use a lame to snitch,
to give you the label of dangerous.
Newspapers say the strangest shit,
it gets eaten up,
by the politicians who be leading us,
War on gangs and blacks ya'll,
we'd pack the jails,
put the war on tax fraud.
I rely on the taken,
my people who are good,
jump through the fire
just to make it.
Lying and faking,
to land a bum deal,
people in the house,
can't tell how the sun feel.
I speak for the majority,
not the few who's paid,
who see the heat,
then reach for designer shades,
A.C buttons, and leading the rat race,
generations of be nothings,
coming in last place,
The principles on poles,
poor need rich,
rich need poor,
and a lie need truth,
like wine need proof,
gotta be smart,
and a little fool,
then nobody can ever use your heart as a tool...
I'm the movement,

the motion,
Chemistry,
the potion of life,
oceanly deep,
my sword is the light,
My brain scopes it all,
my eyes staring,
your not focused at all.
We beefin with the Pharroh,
who got his finger on the trigger,
our face on the barrel,
trying to blow us away...
Actual Indeed,
I know the science on the Easter and the Ex-Mas,
Horses and the headless,
the war for the oil,
Corporation Texas,
Tariffs and treaties,
Columbus and his soliders,
The Caribs and Tainos,
Cabinet Committees,
War on guns got us,
carrying the semi's,
and the war on drugs,
got us bagging up 50's
with no scale,
no bags,
no distribution charge.
All the above, mental pollution or,
what we left to do?
Some get none,
some get a lil,
some get the residue,
Are we law breakers,

outlaws, economy drainers,

poverty claimers,

as the politics paint us?

I've arrived at a new arrival,

preachers already ran through the bible,

new survival techniques are needed,

all crops are weeded,

minds defeated,

stand up now,

but in time be seated...

I'm the movement,

the motion,

Chemistry,

the potion of life,

oceanly deep,

my sword is the light,

My brain scopes it all,

my eyes staring,

your not focused at all.

We beefin with the Pharroh,

who got his finger on the trigger,

our face on the barrel,

trying to blow us away...

Mathematics

This shit is crazy, it's mesmerizing, but it's love

I'm lost in the moments, I'm tortured by the situation, but I excited with the lust.

Is this an equation to be solved, or a fraction to be reduced?

Whatever it is, I was never good at math.

When I try to do right it seems wrong,

The devilish offense is winning, but we're only in the first quarter.

My sight is blurred, but yet so focused on you,

Bitches, lies, and snitches surround our every word,

But our mental - beyond the average sentence,

So, I say we have a chance,
a pace,
a way.
Frustrated at the distance,
But strong as a follower of a knight.
I miss you, when I should be with you
I want you like I should have you
I need you, when I should feel you
I deserve you, as you do me.
These words are distorted, these thoughts are intertwined,
But a reflection of my mind is a portrait of my calculated madness.

Wrapped Up

I should've left you when I doubted you, us, it, then.

I should've took yield when I realized the direction my life was headed.

Headed for disaster, devastation of my human soul.

Never wanting this for myself, always wanting to be the butterfly that flourished in the lands of the greatest.

Silent escapes, impeded by your crawls.

Imprisoned minds is all I see, my reality has escaped me, displaying that I am not in tune with society,

I envision my escape from your demands, your lies, your ties, your truths.

I hate that I hate you for allowing me to hate myself.

Hating my one true existence. Hating that I no longer know what happiness is,

Not knowing how to love,

Being that I wasted my energy pleasing you, falsely: Temporary enjoyment is all you provide. Never really making my insides roar.

Your ways are far from extravagant; original is all that is perceived.

Low classes by the dozen flock in your direction, naming you the king of their lonely kingdom.

Always wanting more for myself, never visioning that I would be a part of society's mockery class.

You're beneath me, and no I don't feel bad to feel such ways about your existence.

You fucked, sucked, and produced out of lust, sorrows, loneliness, and ignorance.

A man with a home monitors the bitches he fucks and situations he produces, so he knows what to present to his home.

A dog, astray is what you are, I tried to tame you, only resulting in a rabbis filled bite. I stick around telling myself different lies to remain in place, but I know that I'm done,

so gone, filling this timeless space with kisses, hugs, and phone calls, only to result in my back being turned to you.

Never wanting to see your ugly inner face.

Never wanting this for anyone else, especially thyself.

You were a true error in my life and I will not allow you to consume me any longer.

Interpretation

Bring meaning out or bring meaning to,

Construe, Concoct, or brew,

Who knew?

The language of the people,

Their culture, and the customs,

How they got married,

Ancestors, the authors,

Mumbo Jumbo was your language, it means ignorant ritual,

Interpreters sold all the rich in you.

Disrobed, and drove us, mentally mowed us down,

Now are authors our echoes?

We interpret language just like the gecko without the insurance or assurance.

Atlantic currents, and Amistad was case for insurance, needs that warrant!

Interpreted your God, smothered you,

Asphyxiated, assiduously toiling through your head,

Mystic making, and mutilate,

Interpret, if you worship, the crown and the queen,

Or do you hear drums in your dreams, lungs giving screams from the bow,

Do you bow and acknowledge colonialism?

I'm never polished.

No treaty or treatise, or empiricist work can restore the faith where cynicism lurks.

No certitude or creed, nor convicted belief, can be trusted authority when ethics are weak.

Just a sheet of paper, piece of tree, interpretation give it the weight and give it wings.

Just an idea, a thought or dream,

Interpretation gives it force and the means.

The awe in the theme.

Trillions of years and ideas, submerged in the Thames,

Lost forever is the price of the Exchange.

Priced the priceless, interpretation concocted, disrupted the rhythm, fathered un-prosodic.

Round 2

I hate that I hate you.

Yeah, I hate you.

I hate everything about you:

Your smile, I'd die for,

Your lips, I yearned to kiss,

Yeah, I hate it all.

Our past relations, I loved, cuz it reminded me of my youth.

Yeah, I hate that too.

I hate that you've made me hate myself.

I hate you, I hate that you've made me hate once again.

May 10, 2010, 10:54am (Actual)

I know your aroma,

Your walk, ya statuesque aura,

Ya prawns and loudness, peaks and ya mountains.

The things you doubt,

The coins, I'm counting,
Throw'em in our bank, ya dreams, our fountain.
Tell me who else struck gold this millennium?
Everyday is a phalanx, hostility planks,
And secrets. Who lies the deepest,
Who is the cheapest, who the weakest,
Who is she thinking of, is he cheating?
Fuck a reason!
I want to be the air in her lungs,
Cure ya bronchi.
Crest you, bless you, near a fire place,
Blockbuster night, skin-a-max,
The Lionsgate is open!
I'm political, with proverbial dialogue,
You're a Shakespearean monologue,
Am I the frog, cause you're a princess?
Calm me down when I'm intense,
Speak ya native tongue, I'm enchantedly entranced.
Sometimes I grasp, sometimes things slip away,
Sometimes I'm on point, sometimes I miss a day.
Your mystic ways and different shades,
Any answers pointed at me ricochet,
Ripped away from common sense.
Can't wash love off if you got the stench,
Everybody turn judge when they get the bench.
We like a fingerprint, the world's a nail salon,
If you don't mimic the patterns doesn't mean you're wrong.

To The Crowd

Don't get the crowd, for I will and shall upset them,
My thoughts I'm sure are contrary to their votes,
I plan to impact the masses,
My voice is a weapon of destruction.
Conceal it, confine your emotions they aren't welcomed in this world
of cattle-ism,

"Speak, speak, let it be heard," "It's written in our rights!" I confer, hearing echoes, as no one is in sight,

Prisoner of my thoughts, individuality got me divided, isolated, desolated,

Okay, Okay, hear, I go again.

You listen closely to refute my pains, ridicule my sacrifices,

How dare thee conjure a false interpretation to fit your flavor?

You selfish bitch, sole being within,

I progress.

My replicated Radical Laryngectomy will ensure you recall these moments.

Be sure not to beg nor plea, for I will return the support provided during my bluntness.

Until that time, project as loud as you may,- I now know, like the rest, you lack true tone.

Masterplan

Is it writer's block, brain freeze,
tall trees, strange leaves,
insane breeds, no pleas!
Seeing things out,
Escort, Cautious!
Don't wanna be dead,
cell floor, nauseous.
Never made it home,
orphan, often...
Thinkin of a Masterplan to get lost in!
Many years muted, dreams,
inaudible.
Lonely is so heavy, but light,
portable.
Breeze like autumn dew,
sneakers never laced, feelings on my sleeves,
I'm going on my eighth!
Grieved cause I'm peeved,

but stand strong,
porcelain.
Thinking of a Masterplan to get lost in!
Eyes, no pupils,
professors, no pupils,
lessons, no tutors,
but my scruples so truthful!
Cops will shoot you,
system will loot ya.
Suffocation or poison,
way of a snake.
With the weight of the world,
my shoulders should break.
A break from the world,
my shoulders could rest,
with a piece of my coffin,
Thinkin of a Masterplan to get lost in!

Love

My elevated, willful comprehension of you,
Love,
has deep seeded, extended and heated, blood!
We used to be tough as fuck,
now we no longer pups, wut up?
My elevated willful comprehension of your love,
has deep seeded , extended and heated,
my sentiments are defeated.
The taste isn't filling,
I'm reluctant to eat it.
Don't agree with this face,
never saw it before,
I equate it with hate!
Sweet turns sour,
who created that fate?
You hate what you loved,

plus loving to hate.
Air tight bliss,
until something escaped .
Maybe in the toilet,
do you equate it to waste?
Wait...
Make a list,
the good and the bad.
The bad goes first,
luggage bag to the purse,
the crabs, all the jerks,
plus the males you dealt with,
your closet is too fragile to shelf shit.
I need a nurse,
someone alert ,
see symptoms,
someone's hurt,
sweeter than some desserts.
Faulty lines is where we built our estate.
So, every time I wake, I pray it doesn't quake.
But, before I sleep, I pray I don't awake.
I harvest for many seasons,
Mrs. Dash is fucking leaving,
out of business, mental fitness has murdered itself.
On trial , I'm the only witness.
I don't wanna harbor,
just wanna sail.
I know the price,
want a sale.
The vivid lights are looking pale.
Follow my words,
arrive at my thoughts.
Check in your heart,
if it's clear, move on Embark!

Just like trees, leave.
Look for the fruits.
Clean through the facts,
get to the roots.
Who rejected, designed deception coups?
Tied your progress,
the knots of a noose.
Contaminated your keynote,
all your values rewrote,
since the day you met him,
you've been sliding down a ski slope.
With every problem, there's a solution.
Cure a symptom,
let the root live-, that's living ruthless.
Truth is, you've no bite,
you're toothless, can't say shit.
And nothing in your head matters,
it's just grey shit.
Your mind can't focus,
It strays fast,
running down the sole of your Asics,
Chasing Love!
Don't try to complicate the Basics: One plus one doesn't need notation.
Climb through the hole, or live in a cage with-,
sorrow and defeat.
No pardons to the weak.
My elevated comprehension is accurate,
not a product of arrogance, or happenstance!

Stopwatch

Dedicated, fractionated, confused, wanting this shit to be over.
You can't be serious, got me waiting like a time clock stuck on eternity.
Appeals, lawyers, letters, operators, c.o.'s, I'm pissed.
Bitches confirm your stay is temporary.

Annoying the shit out of me, as I realize they are conscious.

Suspended in the past, not seeing the moving cars, years, laughs, people, notions, and experiences.

Bursts of the truth send a frightening roar echoing throughout my veins. Ahhhhhhh! It hurts.

Silent cries, no one wants to listen.

My tale- solely entertainment,

others glance, often pierce me with their gazes.

How the fuck?

What's her deal?

I say nothing, leaving you to their imagination.

I've been slaughtered, someone get the aide.

I'm angry,

What the fuck happened and when?

How the fuck did I land here and why have you captured my mere existence?

You knew of your goal, as you are a one-man team.

Share the plans, let her know.

The ideal survivor, product of a gamble.

Is it too late to cash-out?

-Fuck...wait there's an understanding.

Shelling the Man

New love,

True love,

Daydream, I stare into the blue love.

My dew love, natural mist,

Saddled my arrogance,

Crashed my conceit!

I'm nauseous, nautical miles,

No porting,

So awesome!

Oh, how the best things in life are free.

Oh, how I wasted so much time investing in "things."

Mutable trends,

Dogmatist friends,

Depreciated life,

Styled with lifestyles of foolhardys'

You're my howsoever,

My Malcolm quote: By Any Means

My scope,

Your intrusion,

Rendered me ineffective.

You're Half-French,

I'm remonstrating against everything I thought or knew.

Can you repatriate me- to the place I'm from?

I'm stranded, lost,

At a cross between my experiential fact bank, and my inability to match mate!

Balancing means,

Denuding or tipping,

My gauntlet covered bands,

Finding answers in the sands of a clogged hour glass.

I'd follow a yenta, If she spewed out hope, To cope with my---New Love, True Love, Daydream, I stare into the blue love,

Cream of my dew,

Ahhh, Love...

Hidden Treasure

Disappointment after disappointment, wondering how to handle it well,

A professional failure- is the accomplishments I attain.

Minimum deceptive solutions succumb my inner being in so many ways.

Placing real blame on the causes of my errors,

Deterrence- from the truth leads me further from actualization.

Mistaken identity- I'm no longer the woman I used to be.

Distorted values, angry motivates, false personas, torn friendships, distant, disillusioned.

Confidence has subsided, yearning to blend in the shadows.

The star of a discontinued sitcom,
Laughing at the woman I once was, as I imprinted my own footprints.
Follow them not,
Useless to the wise woman of defiance.

Pave the way for the young to emulate, never wanting your name to be mentioned in shame, followed by "however" conjunctions.

Let it stand in solitary, never relying on fortunes to carry the burden of fame.

I have devastated the temple, not acknowledging the disciples to come.

I beg of thee to find what's real, know its worth---beneath the piles of life's burdens, shield your chastity:

IT is tamed, waiting for your discovery,
A true gem.

Untitled

I haven't written a poem in such a long time.
Thinking of your birthday has made me rise to the occasion.

Not wanting to neglect this situation, I decided to analyze your rare traits:

Smiling and laughing draws many to your charisma.

Your disregard for time-- endlessly engaging and entertaining the lust that penetrates my inner thighs.

You are such a woman's man, always wanting to dominate the uncertainties that I fear.

Protecting those lives of dependence is your sole priority.

A continuous learner, who is always prepared to teach.

Acknowledge your strengths, and be thankful for the man that you have become. Realize that a true man grows from within ----with every struggle, every pride check, and every ambiguous task.

Tishel

Winners sometimes lose,
But losers never win a thing!
You will win, you will fly,
I gave you wings.
The chance to see marigolds,

Free to be any role, achieve any goal,
The world is yours.
The chance for me to shower you,
My only girl.
Stand tall tower through every road.
Many things will be said,
Several things will be heard,
Within you is the truth when the world is absurd.
I can't put everything in words,
Or explain the nerve,
You have to just take and learn.
I waited for you,
And weighted by you, even hated for you.
I'll separate, and dedicate myself to your delicate needs.
Prepare you for the sunny people, cold shoulders, and people that breeze.
Prepare you for the Seas, and introduce you to the deserts.
When you struggle through the seasons, know it's just some weather.
The sun's little flower,
No matter how bad it seems,
It's only twenty-four hours.
- Daddy

Baby Blues

How do I handle sickness?
Must I, grapple cough?
Try to laugh it off?
Or, stand by in shame?
You get needles,
I cry in pain.
Please give me the name,
Of whoever never got sick.
And, please show me the parents who had no medical trips.

Admitted

Tricia Lorquet-Monk 10/31/1985 26 yrs 3 months and x amount of days, reads the bracelet on my wrist in the ER.

Admittance number two in two years.

The spans are getting closer,

Fans have departed.

Solitary confinement in sight of strangers.

Unknown glances,

propaganda smiles, selling the false patchwork of healthcare assurance.

Disgusted, disguised; I'm no longer the being make-up, once reflected.

In the hands of foreigners, test-dummy coined.

Needles, IV's, fluids, oh how successful Parkes and Baekeland have become.

Isolation, bedsores, night after night, no calls, no visits, just the two of us, battling for victory.

The Feeble Light

Seeing the changes evolve in sight is so devastating. Never expecting the worst- now living its reality.

Motivation to transcend evaporated like the thin summer breeze we once enjoyed.

The idea of sitting on the benches, rehearsing the name of our unborn child is as foreign as the thought of you putting the green weeds and blunt wrap to your lips.

Seeing the changes got me tripping. Matter of fact, I've fallen; Not wanting to rise only to be approached with the life that has abandoned me, forsaken me for the envious "green" ways of my past.

Please allow me the chance to retract. I promise I've learned:

To listen to my elders,

Use mistakes as lessons,

Take life in healthy strides,

Create a path to be followed- oppose to avoided.

Despite the apparent mess of inevitable change, I sit in sorrow-- seeing, ignoring, - the changes.

I'm shattered, the pieces off at sea. How will I be repaired? Yearning for assistance, in a resisting manner, left to negotiate my make-up for reinvention.

He has lost. Is lost. Yet guiding us.

Will they be found?

The 35 Year-Old Runaway

The black man is missing once more.

Where are the Toussaints, and Dessalines to shake their heads in disgrace?

Protecting a nation, race for mankind.

Cutting heads with swords to save the purity of the black women's natural treasures.

Pure land, pure morals.

The black man was present more than ever.

Showing his strength,

an arm of iron,

tongue of steel,

strike of fire,

The black man was a presence to be in.

Negotiations, compliments, threats, and treachery, leading to the victory of freedom.

The black man ever so present.

So proud were mothers, daughters, wives, and aunts,

standing to see the black man's stride,

standing tall for his beliefs, his nation, his heritage, his future-

the black man was strong.

Too strong for his opponents, only to be fooled.

Too wise and confident for his own good.

Oh, how strong was he.

Body builds of lust.

Desiring the black man, was an inevitable cause.

His family unit remained solid, setting the standards for his time.

The black man was present, I felt his worth.

Interweaving everlasting treaties in the land's quilt work.

Demanding listeners and standing ovations.

Yeah, the black man was strong.

His strength didn't vanish at sea, with false intentions; it coasted the sea, spreading throughout the nations of black men, reaching the Quakers' land.

The black man's toils didn't go unanswered.

He sacrificed but remained strong-

Until that day he held the white flag, surrendering himself, family, daughters, sons, brothers, and mothers.

The black man was defeated.

His strength undone,

Coined-" the 35 year old runaway" by the single mother of two.

A Prisoner's Longing

Boon are your handcuffs,

On my wrist,

My wrist would be slit,

If you let me go.

Flow out every drip,

No safety valve switch.

Dead to my peers,

Dead to my fears, all have confirmed now.

Dead to and through years, which way is home now?

No watch,

No clock,

Call and tell me of the times I left at airports, beaches, at bars, and weekends afar.

All I know is weekend enjoyments are far.

Damn! I miss my kids.

Tickle their ribs,

Pickle their brain with thoughts of me home.

Daddy in the room, mom in the kitchen,

Or daddy in the kitchen, mom always bitchin.

Our spice of life,

Season our own way.

Things I miss,

I miss them all day.

To Be or Not to Be?

Would they kill Jesus if he wasn't revolutionary?
If he concurred with the spiritual crime of the times?
Would they have impaled him to the pine?
Clearly they'd burn down his house,
If he had a home,
Or challenge him to a debate,
If they had the stones.
Jesus roamed through Rome,
Homeless in one way,
At home in another.
He didn't glut at the last supper,
Walked on waters that were angry with waves,
The only words he spoke were, "don't be afraid..."
His theme,
Breaks traditions,
Cut from the seam, or fabric of false alignment and uncleanliness.
The gumption of heaven, consumption, relationship, and hell sparsely stained with unhappy have-nots.
You should own the field that heaven and happiness are buried in.
Don't fear standing out.
Bold acts become miracles,
As quick as the view change.
Some call him Christ,
Others call him insane.

Pasar Una Noche en Blanco

Many nights,
I toss and turn
for a small moment of sleep!
Linked and looped through dimensions.
I blink!
Eyes adjust to the darkness,
to lighten the confusion.
Thinking convoluted,

works great, means straight, within my circuitous mind.
Seasoned and fried,
in the ghetto's kitchen,
pour from poverty's pot!
To hot to consume,
to sick to plague!
Cleaned in the tub, where misery bathes.
I pray,
to a calendar,
asking for better days.
I opened every door and stoked the devil's maze.
Amazed,
this page of life is invisible ink.
It riddles my reach,
as my ability leaks,
out of my pores and my heart pores out in heaps.
Many hours I toss and turn for just a moment of some sleep!

Gizzy Loves the Women

He loves women, so many, one man. They fulfill all his needs, fulfilling the

void; a mother--- he never knew.

He summits himself for the moment, only to capture you, his prey.

No identity, no DNA, a Nomad, content with his lifestyle, despite the hurt others feel. Protectiveness of him is worthless, he's no prize.

Sorrow fills me for the moment, devastated that my dream hasn't come true.

Why is happiness so selective?

I raise my hand hoping to get called. I guess it's not my turn.

I have a few more years to go... I contemplate not.

He caused hurt.

His little wonders are alone to find their father. A guide to let them know they are shielded.

Be that one; Do that correctly.

He loves women, has two daughters to build into the ideal women.

Evolving Time

Waiting for time to evolve,

These moments are memories soon to dissolve. Waiting patiently, unable to precisely perceive the motions at hand. Indivisibly bias is the truth of the present. Baby mothers, single fathers, wed-locked children, chasing dick, a constant strive. When will the barrel break, and time evolve?

Restless in "saving every cent." The Haitian Dream, turned to the American Dream, and retracted back to my Deferred Dream. I'm dried up, washed up, tired of hoping and waiting for him to evolve. Evolve into the man of my imagination, the man who she begs for mercy. Evolve already.

You read this and speculate my inner thoughts. Don't. I speak them clearly. I'm saddened, angered, betrayed, hated, and revengeful of time. I want it to move s-l-o-w-l-y during the good times, and Evolve! during times as such.

Young kids, beating on each other--- females, males, and the elder. I'm nervous, having to build a shield, yielding, everyone to stay away. The hard exterior has converted into my interior. A self-made beast, stay away! Until time evolves, I am me. Tongue sharper than any machete he can find in the remote areas of Les Cayes. The pains of life have raised me. Battered women, men's fist, unseen tears---escape me! leave my mind to itself. Would –you—please- evolve?

Evolve to the unknown. Evolve to distant lands of luxury, beauty, payments, and folklores. Evolve to my ideal utopia. Endless pleasure, familiar faces, and time at our disposal. Let it not be in death for one to know his or her true worth. Know that time has waited and evolved for you solely. Understand that time of deception leads to appreciation of authenticity. Until then... I patiently wait, loudly, for Time to Evolve.

Authenticity

Give me a neighborhood decorated with graffiti, because it means inspirations are amidst

Give me hair salons filled with different dialects, it keeps my roots alive

Give me culture inspired restaurants, because it lets me know my dreams may actualize.

Give me the corner fights; they let me know self-pride still exists.

Give me the unique extensions, as I resemble my African tribes.

Give me a curvy body, they let me know I'm childbearing.

Give me a tongue sharper than a machete, lets you know not to fuck with me.

Routes

Where do I find the strength to go on?

Been defeated so many times,

Conquered yet I still walk.

My legs and rhythm automatically beating to their own drum.

I know it's dumb, rhetorical to wonder the motivation, but I am curious, suspicious of the human mind.

Told to seat down, to longer make a sound.

Becoming an outer shell of my true identity, never wanting to display my inner strength I fear of your approval.

Where do my thoughts find the avenue to thrive, aspire, and explore? The road is dusted, far from paved, understanding the trails it has taken to land me here.

Yet in great distraught with struggles that still bear.

When will my heart synch with my soul? When will my destiny follow my passions? When will I bear contentment? Backwards roller coaster ride got me tripping. I know this isn't my path. It doesn't feel right, too uneasy to know where to sit.

I'm visiting different stations, never finding my seat.

Tickets half-purchased, wanting to explore different routes.

Walking through, straight through.

You tried.

Tried aggressively to defeat me.

My heart, my legs, my soul, beat to their own original drum.

The drum of my ancestors. The drums of Africa. The drums of warriors, the ones that made their way, defined it, and past it on for inheritance.

I'm more than the physical, I'm all I know nothing of. So, for you whom tries to conceal me, STOP! I will succeed.

Succeed all your doubts and all my dreams.

I know where I'm coming from, so the going is even easier.

Thanks to God.

~My conscience

HIS PRIDE

HE made me big, proud, and Black

To bear a life of turmoil, led by persuasion,

HE made me big, proud, and Black.

I sit often contemplating HIS motives of delivering his child into poverty, sorrow, and shear madness. But, my eyes see, never to touch. My ears hear, only to learn and recollect. My heart pumps fear- fear for me, them, they, us. I'm fearful daily, smile rarely.

HE made me big, proud, and Black

Black like the inhabitants of the lonely Caribbean Sea, holding the dreams, stories, and defeats of many. Black like the imprints of the historical accounts, of the masses, masses of cattle cargo Africans- chained, whipped, ignored, voiceless in the dark nights of their Blackness. An empty vessel, no see-through, pointless, like the life so many live.

HE made me big, proud, and Black

Big, big like the towers that rule the streets, and alleyways of Manhattan. Like the King of the Highways. Big. Hips designed to take in a true black man, with all his gifts. Big. Big to bear the fruits of my labor. Big. Big to defeat the envious thoughts and mutters that fill a room of my presence.

He made me big, proud, and Black.

So, when the world requests a big proud beautiful Black woman to bow her head of disgrace, stand taller than the towers, put your hands on those curvious hips, and whine, whine, whine, whine like the island girls of the Caribbean, forgetting about all the sorrows of the time. Enjoy yourself, the moment of mere existence.

He made you big, proud, and Black.

Amen

Body

I had a dream one December

I was able to converse with my body, I remember.

Asking eyes if they've seen love

And-

If water is thicker than blood?

Water said,"Without me blood couldn't sail."

I asked heart about love, he said go to mind.

Mind was distracted and asked for some time.

So I asked touch if it felt love,

"Maybe," he said.

"Maybe when I was innocent...a baby."

He was unsure, Maybe thought I said Pure.

I repeated the question, he said "Awaken brain from snore."

Leaving touch, going to brain, where he sent me.

There was holes and patches in this area called memory.

The sky, there, gray, clouded with calm.

I asked, "Are you brain?" Out his mouth came a fog.

It lingered in the air of my personal space.

His mechanical voice said "You're at the right place."

"I heard your question because I record everything different from Mind, who puts importance on things."

"Unfortunately for you, I've recorded various answers, I've heard love in song and various anthems."

"Smelled it behind closed doors, as you were gasping the power, sweat and sweet air--- love was passion."

"Tasted it at those Sunday church dinners."

Best dish award, Love was the winner.

"Seen in the likes of your wife,"

"She gave you her life to ease your strife."

"Before this dream ends, here's a question for you..."

"What makes love so confusing for you?"

I said, "I thought something solid couldn't have melted."

"Now it's hard to believe I have ever felt it."

"You deal with what you're dealt with, because you heard, tasted, seen, and smelled love."

I awoke, called to tell my wife about my nightmare last night. I said that my whole body said that I'm in love with my wife.

White Noise

White noise begins at the Office, State Executive,
A large map on the wall, the Governor searching the nakedness.
White noise turns into Laws, the Legislature looking to hire some dedicated farmers.
White noise uses the Judicial Court System, that makes slaves by treating the poor different.
White noise is in the eyes of the average applicant, who only wants to beat, kill, and chain up Africans.
White noise is their abuse of discretion.
White noise enforces senseless rules.
White noise sounds like marching steps and metal keys.
White noise is screaming in a phone "baby please!"
What noise is racism, the color is skin.
White noise is no cornrows or beards on your chin.
White noise didn't let her visit because her clothes was too tight.
White noise let her visit simply because he was white.
White noise, the dissolution of hard-shelled social skills.
White noise is tons of desire minus all the will.
White noise is when murderers and robbers are judgmental.
White noise is womanizers sending letters and sentimentals.
White noise turns into court dates,
Living out your worst fate.

I Lied: My Truth

The first time I lied, was back in the day.
See, beatings made me cry, I had to find a way.
Nobody appeared to care, as long as it didn't hear THEM.
Everything was cool, and everyone were friends.
I lied about my home, its address and all.
Made people believe they were better, but I was better at ball.
I lied about my family. My existence in deadweight-- ROCKLAND.
Really, I'm Harlem, Rockland only-- via an ugly adoption.

Told rappers they were good, though really trash.

Made the suburban kids think they were tough, yet I knew they were ass.

I'd fake, then throw a punch, then shout "one-on-one!"

I did it often, to avoid getting jumped.

My friends taught me voodoo, during Catholic School Days

On day I said, "I'm God." They all went berserk.

Told mom, I loved her, never really did.

I never felt love until I hugged my first true kid.

I'm loud, and reckless. Inside I'm really shy.

I wait, and calculate to seize the perfect time.

I make future plans, but don't wanna live another day.

I expand my mind, but live the same way.

You lie to yourself at night, and call'em dreams.

Our difference is operation, design, and scheme.

Hear my truth within.

LIFE

Scorched by stress, die hair follicle.

Life , tastes like a straight shot,

of Russian water,

historically distilled,

vitriol within the mouth,

violently washing soft tissue,

of the freshmen and untoddy.

Life, feels like wrinkles on young faces,

chiseled by worriment,

helpless, unhopeful,

visibly beaten between forbearance and lust,

violently starving the vigor,

of the guilty and innocent.

Life, smells like airproofed despair a,

fire on flesh,

no smoke,

unbathed urban borough'd cocktail,

violently mixing the cultures,
of the disobedient and civics.
Life, looks like Manfred on Jungfrau,
like optional suicide,
snow squalled,
vie Vying for daily recrudesce,
violently staying alive,
of the pitiful and wild.
Life, sounds like a steel hell,
cold steel bars,
keys, echos
inaudible screams atop lungs,
violent kicks, stomps, punches,
of the body and soul,
Black Men and Women wither in the way of the old.

Burden

Many, many years,
Hearing your voice,
But, not seeing your face,
Just your commode!
Your eyes brought fear to my life,
If ever exposed,
Down the commode!
Kipling's* Burden was heedlessly robust,
Full of physical harm.
So, my eyes went straight from your commode,
To your arms.

* Rudyard Kipling, author of a late 1800 poem titled "White Man's Burden," speaking of the task the white man has to "civilize"...others. A position which suggests that all non-white men are not civilized and beneath that of the white man.

These ideas developed abou non-whites were popular and lead to more writings, led to white men believing it was their responsibility to civilize in any manner they felt, and to other sciences, like Eugenic clinics throughout the city. Thus, many Black Men were murdered, by any and for any means.

Profit-Air

Unreasonable profits have been made,
Through an enslaved sweaty wage.
Through caged intellectual capacity,
The swallowing process of capitalization,
Sickened at the sigh, a choking profiteer.
Choking on profit, and the profundities of his profit center.
Deficient in decency,
From first endorsement to position of regency.
The inner-city poor blinded by allure and binded in stores.
Hoping to fly high, make a mark, a stamp, finish the fifty, a trophy, or a ring,
But lacing up his sneakers is like building Sing-Sing!
But, lace up your sneakers,
And pray for the jackpot,
Cause he prays your ass gets locked up in a cement box.
And, remember, he's a champ,
Champions never lose.
If you want to win, don't buy his shoes.
Retreat, don't attend his camps, his functions,
And don't wear his clothes.
His goals are unlike yours,
He's a defense contractor that likes wars,
He's the gun in the knife fight,
The drop of poison in the Christmas dinner, the hard price!
Clandestine!
The chauffeur to a prison cell,
A black face living well,
Fooling those who supported'em and don't give a hell!
What's lower than the cost to make his goods?
The price of his soul,
Black as if a piece of coal had cancerous lungs.

Black like the mask at the opera on the phantoms' face.
Blacker than Jim Crow's legacy.
Blacker than the inner-city.
Blacker than a dark night in jail.
Profiteer gambling to make money don't fail!

Neo-Social Manifestos

Take everything that you hear,
Set it on fire!
Go online, and call the Pope, Prez, or Priest a liar: Press Send.
Argue with everyone--all your friends,
Sue both your parents,
Ignore what's apparent,
Unleash all belief and let it blend.
Create your own world,
Name it,
Take a hundred self pictures-a day,
Be famous.
When things go bad,
Blame it, ...on your past!
Be heard, not seen. Text, don't speak.
Speak what you hear, not what you see.
Be that cutting edge thing,
Live your 20's theme.
That image silver screen,
The female angry, awkward, and curve.
The envied male,
Use each word, get'em jealous.
Be the empty-headed human ,
Be thin-skinned, easily stirred like, starved boxed lion,
Sentimental when technology is on, though dry crying.
Find a lane for your brain,
And let go.
Embrace these Neo-Social Manifestos.

BONUS POEMS

New York Nights

Nights in New York are cold....bundle up, it's going to be a real one.

Your eyes gotta stay woke, cause niggas will take you for a joke, take you for that ride, may end up losing ya life.

Nights in New York are cold, ... bundle up, it's going to be a real one.

Night terrors leaving chills running through ya spine; the realities we hear outside. .... mother's aborting newborns in the dumpsters, alleyways ... brothers, fathers, sons, and uncles, losing their lives-- forced into contemporary slavery.

Nights in New York are cold, ... bundle up, it's going to be a real one.

Thinking of a move.. mind spinning, hoping for a better chance. RIP the "New York" label off, looking towards a lighter coat, lighter load.

Nights in New York are cold, got my mind fucked all the way up. Niggas grinding for self ... the realest state got the most heart to leave you floating dolo.

Nights in New York are cold, ... bundle up, it's going to be a real one.

An African-American Bedtime Tale

An African-American Bedtime Tale

Red, burgundy, or a plain tee shirt? Which color should I wear? "I want the crowd in awe upon my entrance ." Iron, iron, board, starch, spray the cologne, for the night must start.

Pick out your favorite book, "not too long, for it's bedtime." Princess, sorcerers, and Princes-to-the-rescue.

Friday nights looking for a parking spot on the busy streets, lights, bumpers, honks. Right next to the spot, oh how ideal.

"Mommy, may I please have some milk? I believe I've become thirsty just after using the bathroom, and oh after the milk, before the story, I need to get my favorite teddy to join." Patiently waiting for the tasks of the night to unfold, prior to the end in sight.

Out the whip, "is that him? He's here, he's here." Slow walks in search of familiar faces, and faces to place on reserve. "What's up?" "What's good?" "chilling, chilling."

"Alright girls, off to bed" warm tucks and kisses, assuring that the night's darkness is only in the temporary presence, as colorful dreams will be sure to surpass. Pick up the final toys, put clothes away, clean the kitchen and bathroom before the night's end.

"This is my tune!" Dances, drinks, tugs, and air kisses, in the waves of the night. Playing cat and mouse for the few hours that remain.

All the house labors are done. Shower, perfumes, lingerie, awaiting his cumming, as she silently drifts to sleep.

Daddy's home __7am. Mommy awakes to prepare breakfast and hopes to one night, get dressed, feel beautiful, and mistily enjoy the night lights, replicating her husband. She whispers in their ear, "daddy is home from work, he's sorry he missed our bedtime tale."

A Mother's Guide to SEE

Loving her is mandatory. She requires time, and space. My little ocean-wide, mind and heart. She demands her respect, though portraying a tiny vessel. She defines and defies fierceness, making a mockery of the term.

Expanding your realm of reverence, results from her company,

In all. I yearn to deliver my zest, wisdom, and love to her. Protection from the bare arms of others---mere strangers.

Walk through life the way you are. Your own mother tirelessly tries to shape you, change you, and train you, according to her liking;

You resist, smart beyond your years.

Be you. Never silenced, never stereotyped, but immortalized.

Stay in health. Take genuine, lite breaths, from the challenges and accomplishments of life. Surface; face your SEA with dominance and TELL the world your presence is inevitable.

INDEX BY tITLE

About the Author

"Focused, enlightened, and educated... A Writer to the core."

When sentenced to two concurrent 15 year prison terms, with no biological family, and surrounded by fake friends, you quickly rely on God, love, and your girlfriend for survival. Your girlfriend-turned wife, in turn, relies on God, love, and poetry to see the bid through. Herein, is the tale of both experiences, and observations during the 15-year prison sentence, in NYS maximum security prisons.

You get to hear the stories, humanize the outcasts of society, build life-long friendships, and engage in supernatural divinely guided love that only a small group of prison wives and husbands conceptualize.

This collection of poetry candidly focuses on the human experience in America's 20th century prison system: minority disenfranchisement, inferiority, racism, discrimination, love, parenthood, mass incarceration, "broken-homes", trauma, poverty, sexulaity, growth, and spirituality all interwined in harmonious literary form.

www.ingramcontent.com/pod-product-compliance
Lightning Source LLC
Chambersburg PA
CBHW060356130626
46553CB00003B/1260